I Am a Shark

The Life of a Hammerhead Shark

by Darlene R. Stille illustrated by Todd Ouren

Special thanks to our advisers for their expertise:

Susan H. Shane, Ph.D., Biology
University of California at Santa Cruz

Susan Kesselring, M.A., Literacy Educator
Rosemount-Apple Valley-Eagan (Minnesota) School District

I Live in the Ocean

PICTURE WINDOW BOOKS
Minneapolis, Minnesota

Managing Editors: Bob Temple, Catherine Neitge
Creative Director: Terri Foley
Editors: Nadia Higgins, Patricia Stockland
Editorial Adviser: Andrea Cascardi
Designer: Todd Ouren
Page production: Picture Window Books
The illustrations in this book were prepared digitally.

Picture Window Books
5115 Excelsior Boulevard
Suite 232
Minneapolis, MN 55416
877-845-8392
www.picturewindowbooks.com

Printed in the United States of America.

Library of Congress Cataloging-in-Publication Data
Stille, Darlene R.
I am a shark : the life of a hammerhead shark /
by Darlene R. Stille ; illustrated by Todd Ouren.
p. cm. — (I live in the ocean)
Includes bibliographical references (p.   ).
ISBN 1-4048-0599-0 (reinforced lib. bdg.)
1. Hammerhead sharks—Juvenile literature. I. Ouren, Todd,
ill. II. Title.

QL638.95.S7S75 2004
597.3'4—dc22
                              2004000890

Look at my long, sleek body. Watch me slip silently through the dark sea. I am a shark.

They call me a hammerhead shark.
Can you see why?

A shark is a kind of fish. Sharks are different from most fish because shark bones are made of cartilage. It is the strong, bendable stuff that forms your ears and the tip of your nose.

Swish, swish.

I move my tail from side to side to glide through the water.

Hammerhead sharks swim in warm oceans around the world. They can be found near the shore and out in the open water.

4

The fins on my back and belly keep my body from rolling back and forth. The fins on my sides are for turning and helping me float.

I never stop swimming. I slow down to rest, but I never really sleep. If I stopped moving, my heavy body would sink.

I also swim to keep fresh water flowing over my gills. My gills take oxygen out of the water so I can breathe.

Unlike most fish, sharks don't have an air-filled sac inside their bodies to keep them afloat. They have to keep swimming, or they would sink.

As I swim, I swing my big head back and forth. I am always on the lookout for tasty prey.

I have excellent eyesight. I'm great at spotting fish whizzing by in dark water.

Though sharks have eyelids, most never blink or close their eyes.

My sense of smell is even more amazing. My powerful nose can pick out a single drop of blood in gallons and gallons of water.

Look where my nostrils are—on the ends of my big head. A smell reaches one nostril before it reaches the other one. That helps me figure out where a smell is coming from.

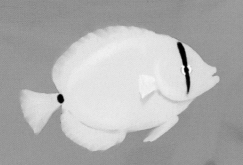

Even though you can't see ears on a shark, the animal also has good hearing. A shark is especially good at hearing low sounds made by sick or injured fish. These fish are easy prey for a hungry shark.